Advance praise for *Far Company*

"Earthly and sidereal, Cindy Hunter Morgan's beautifully realized new book takes memory as its talisman, always mindful that 'the stars watch from long ago.' But 'long-ago' can fade like invisible ink, as when a homemade Halloween costume both erases and silences a girl at her new school, or when warrior paint impishly applied to a mother's face prompts her baffling retreat to the hideout of her sewing room. Given so much disappearance, 'After the Dragonflies' strives 'to see the world in slow motion'; but just as often, Morgan's poems convey the eerie exactitude of time-lapse photography, duration quickened to reveal the world's secret acts of becoming. Time after time, *Far Company* discovers those liminal moments when the unseen shades into vision. Who wouldn't wish to linger there?"

—Steven Cramer, author of *Listen* and *Clangings*

"I simply love the quiet wisdom, the subtle music, the devotion to memory, and how imagination transforms the act of remembering in Cindy Hunter Morgan's poems. As she dwells in her grandmother's orchard—the old house burned to ashes, horses dead and buried—she declaims, 'where does anything go except / into forever.' Following W. S. Merwin as muse, Hunter Morgan has written into the present moment a gorgeous, lyrical celebration of how the long dead live in our bodies, how time collapses and is remade in poems."

—Todd Davis, author of *Native Species* and *Winterkill*

"If you make yourself available to Cindy Hunter Morgan's poems, they will revivify your experience of the most ordinary aspects of everyday life. Layering the childhood fears, wonders, and myths of her imagination in the animal world, she creates a kind of chrysalis for the emergence of a more deeply realized awareness of our present human experience. These poems shine and resonate."

—Dan Gerber

FAR

COMPANY

Made in Michigan Writers Series

GENERAL EDITORS

Michael Delp, Interlochen Center for the Arts
M. L. Liebler, Wayne State University

A complete listing of the books in this series can be
found online at wsupress.wayne.edu.

FAR

COMPANY

POEMS BY
CINDY HUNTER MORGAN

WAYNE STATE UNIVERSITY PRESS
DETROIT

ISBN 978-0-8143-4952-6 (paperback)
ISBN 978-0-8143-4953-3 (e-book)

Library of Congress Control Number: 2021945814

Publication of this book was made possible by a generous gift from The Meijer Foundation.

On cover: *Still Life at Dusk* © Matthew Cusick, 2017. Inlaid maps on panel. Artwork courtesy of Pavel Zoubok Gallery. Cover design by Laura Klynstra.

Wayne State University Press rests on Waawiyaataanong, also referred to as Detroit, the ancestral and contemporary homeland of the Three Fires Confederacy. These sovereign lands were granted by the Ojibwe, Odawa, Potawatomi, and Wyandot Nations in 1807 through the Treaty of Detroit. Wayne State University Press affirms Indigenous sovereignty and honors all tribes with a connection to Detroit. With our Native neighbors, the press works to advance educational equity and promote a better future for the earth and all people.

Wayne State University Press
Leonard N. Simons Building
4809 Woodward Avenue
Detroit, Michigan 48201-1309

Visit us online at wsupress.wayne.edu.

CONTENTS

I

II

III

I

Rain Light

After W. S. Merwin

All day the stars watch from long ago.
I understood this even as a girl,
when my grandma and I played Flinch
on rainy days, our fingertips joining
the fingerprints of her grandparents.
In that way the people she loved
held my hand those afternoons
when hollyhocks pressed their faces
against the porch screens
and horses gathered near the fence
to drink from rain-topped pails,
the pasture thicker every year
with what had already been there
and what hadn't, hickory
and grapevines and burdock,
raindrops beading like sweat
on the lips of snapdragons,
everything green pressing in—
close, my grandma called that weather.

Origin Story

I was six months old, sleeping in an open tent
when a bobcat circled, lingered near the cushion,

near my breath—milk-sweet, warm. His whiskers
tickled my cheek, soft as the belly of a vole.

His haunches brushed my arm. My father
witnessed the incident, then startled the bobcat,

sent it into the woods to sleep or flush a rabbit.
Every parent hands a child over to the world.

I grew as a girl grows, but I wandered creek beds,
built dens in the woods, filled them with the skulls

of foxes and dry oak leaves. Afternoons, I napped
on the edge of meadows beneath aspens or pin oaks,

woke mottled—sunlight and leaf shadows
flickering on my skin—my flesh dappled like fur.

Amulet

That Halloween I was a new girl—first day
at a new school. I could have worn street
clothes, been *the girl nobody knew*, but

I went as a mute clown sewn from a bed sheet—
faded stripes, ruffled collar. My mother made it,
and made my wig—red yarn stitched

to a muslin bonnet. My mother, who took me
to school, left me with a sack lunch and a tube
of lipstick—Revlon's *Cherries in the Snow*—

her only makeup. *For the parade*, she said,
closing her palm over mine. I marched
behind Cleopatra—*Cleopatra*—I thought

that was her name—necklace coiled like a snake,
gold cape like a river—plastic, store-bought,
though I said nothing. Later, we had cupcakes

and fruit punch, then bingo with bottle caps.
At recess, I wandered like a fool, my hands
in the pocket of my costume

until I made it through the gauntlet
of jump ropes and swings into a grove
of maples in the far corner of the playground

and pulled the lipstick tube out—gold, shiny,
hard as the shell of a scarab—
my mother in front of the bathroom mirror

before church, my mother in the grocery
store/shoe store/fabric store—my mother
released to me in wax and red dye.

1978

One day, I paint my mother's face
with rocks—pound dolostone,
basalt, quartzite into powder,

dribble spit into what I crush,
rub paint onto her nose, cheeks,
forehead—every streak one finger

wide. My mother made wild,
glossed with magic. I take a picture,
try to fix her as warrior companion.

I wave the Polaroid like
a smoke blessing, wait for it to dry.
When I look up, she's gone.

Later, I find her in her sewing room—
face washed off, her foot on the pedal
of her machine as though she is driving

our brown Oldsmobile to the milk store.
The windows are open. Streetlights
buzz. It's *Indian summer.*

Heat blurs the trees
into smudged still lifes.
My mother stuffs elastic

into a waistband, sends me to bed.
I lean out my window like a dog.
Bats reel. Rabid. Lucky. I squirm

all night, searching for the cool part
of my cotton sheets, those places
my body has not yet been.

Nuthatch

It's not that I wanted to shoot anything,
but when Billy Blanding showed me
the shoebox with a dead nuthatch,

I thought I was Audubon. I knew
I'd finally *seen* something—
black stripe painted straight through

the eye, belly dipped in cinnamon,
heat radiating from the plump chest.
After that, I still made plaster casts

of fox tracks, but they bored me—
molds of something already gone.
I wanted more birds—soft throats,

wing bars. I took my slingshot into
the orchard, missed a bluebird, missed
an oriole. I found antlers and kept them

for my bookshelf—displayed them
behind a single row of rocks.
But they were hard and cold. I wanted

the warmth of the newly dead, the blue-
tipped wing of the nuthatch—
feathered colors wet like paint.

Mouser

My mother supplied a sawed-off
ladder to climb into the basement
crawl space—damp concrete tomb

three feet high littered with mouse
droppings, which I saw only because
I took a flashlight. I carried the light

to find traps—crept toward them until
I pinched the two long sides—wood,
limp whip of a thin tail curled over

an edge. Then I wriggled out, torch
in one hand, trap in another, until
I breathed again the better air

of the basement and held the mouse
over a brown lunch bag, pulled the kill
bar, released the rodent and closed

my fist around the top of the bag
like I was holding the neck of a Faygo
bottle. For this, my mom paid me

twenty-five cents—quarters I stacked
like poker chips. I was her youngest
child, cheaper than a cat.

Red Suede Shoes

Nine years old and I wanted something
to pet, to put in my lap and take for walks,
companionable and leashed—
four legs trotting beside me,
lure of the almost domesticated.
But we got a gerbil—
quivering, embryonic lump,
whiskers like the legs of a spider,
legs like the thin curves of my mother's eyebrows
she penciled on before church.
My sister and I gave it an orange maze,
a blue Habitrail, a dish of water.
One day, we let it out for a walk in the rain.
It was only in our backyard,
but when we lost it we were desperate.
I found it trembling
beneath a dripping viburnum
and gave it dry cedar shavings, clean water,
a new toy—a ping-pong ball.
I hoped it would see the moon in that ball,
but it was listless, probably fevered.
After three days, my dad put it in a shoebox
and gassed it in the garage.
We buried it beneath the viburnum
and sang Joni Mitchell's "Circle Game"—
her carousel a Habitrail, her carousel
our penance. Later that summer,
before school, we went shopping.
At Shepard's Shoes the salesman
disappeared behind a curtain,
came back with a blue box, winked at me,
opened the lid with the flourish of a magician.
I winced, but the man smiled, pulled out
a pair of red shoes with three stripes—
white laces, the clean rubber
soles of a new school year.
I reached in to stroke the suede toes.

After the Dragonflies

After W. S. Merwin

Dragonflies were as common as sunlight
in that other world we called summer.
I couldn't pull a towel from a dock post
without startling several, couldn't slide
into a canoe without disturbing more.
Little erratic drones, they saw everything.
Some said they could sew your lips shut,
and so I tried not to excite them. I learned
early to let them perch on my head
like barrettes that didn't hold anything.
Mornings in that other time, I drank
coffee on the end of the dock
watching them skim the lake, trying,
like them, to see the world in slow motion.

Two Horses

Wendy stuffed cash in sawed-off
two-liter Coke bottles,

money her dad won at the races,
though I didn't understand

what kind of races.
Horses, she told me, and I thought

of my grandpa's mare, the sugar cubes
I gave her after every ride.

Wendy said there was money in the basement too,
but when we went down we found only popcorn,

foil packages stacked in boxes
behind a bar teetering with liquor.

We ate it in the dark, our fingers
chalked and glowing with powdered cheese,

and talked about what Wendy did
with a boy down the street.

I wanted her to slow down, I wanted
to think about the boy I liked,

the way he put his hand in
my back pocket at the dance,

warm weight of his palm
hiding inside one layer of my jeans,

but Wendy explained too much—
the boy's tongue was sticky, his ears smelled.

Outside, my eyes wrecked,
I cupped my hands around my forehead,

told Wendy I had to go home—
my dad was cutting wood,

I needed to stack it before dinner.
My mom was making pot roast.

Wendy stood blinking, confused, her hair
as thick as a mane, one kernel

caught in her bangs like a burr.
She was a wild-haired girl

stuck in a different pasture,
and I was a girl with a bike

propped against the fence,
sun winking on the handlebars.

Centaur

The Olson boys were not supposed to hunt,
but they snuck in over a stile
in the corner of the pasture,

stalked deer in the margins of the day.
One of them lost an arrow in the woods
and gave up looking. My pony found it—

stepped on it, drove the shaft up her leg
like a nail until it bent,
the fletching dragging behind her

when she limped into the barnyard.
We buried her in the pasture
with all the other dead horses—

Queenie, Archie, Dolly, Ginger—
and walked over her grave every morning
to feed the last horse left.

That spring, when pigweed and orchard grass
spread into her still-soft mound,
I went to the planetarium

where a man drew white lines between stars,
reciting names I'd never remember.
All I had to do was tilt my head back,

stretch my throat beneath that domed sky,
and I was underground,
looking up at bones.

Wormhole

Because French made my tongue heavy—so many vowels, so many afternoons counting pets I did not have, untangling masculine and feminine nouns—I sometimes asked to leave, said I needed to go to the bathroom, said this in English so there could be no misunderstanding. I was sixteen. I took a friend. The French teacher always said yes, though never in English. One day, we found the catwalk above the auditorium and climbed out of the hour. The catwalk led to the costume room, the costume room to the Kit Kat Club, to Salzburg, to River City. We found choruses in the creases of pleated dresses, Maria's lipstick on the lapel of Harold Hill's suit, Fräulein Kost's negligee in Captain von Trapp's pocket, cigarettes in Winthrop's little brown vest, a condom in a nun's habit. We clothed ourselves in barbershop quartets, found the door hidden behind the Wells Fargo wagon, stairs behind the door. Back in the classroom, our peers conjugated sorrow, *je suis désolé, nous sommes désolés, qu'ils sont désolés*—their recitation a skipping rope. I lifted my eyes, Maria in the abbey listening to children outside. Light wiggled in tubes above me, found a way out but never a way back. Harold Hill's aftershave lingered on my fingertips. I kept rubbing my nose, thinking of spats and parasols, white frocks swaying from hangers that jingled like wind chimes.

Romance

We bought Avon for the horses
because it was supposed to keep
flies away. Mornings, I rubbed
Skin So Soft on my mare's neck
until she gleamed. Flies circled
anyway—low hum of their wings
the drone of those days. I leaned
forward in the saddle and flicked
them off, thought of Jack Elam in
Once Upon a Time in the West,
the sweaty close-up of his face,
his bad eye rolling like a marble.
I wanted to catch a fly
in the barrel of a gun. I wanted
a name like *Harmonica.*
That summer I made everything
into a Western—click of fetlock,
boots on gravel, whinny of the mare
left in the pasture. There was
more to this than imagination.
My grandpa's grandpa in Missouri
worked the railroads the same years
Jesse James robbed them. I was that
close to outlaws. I trained my eyes
to find snakes, kept my thighs
squeezed around the saddle.
I smelled of Avon all summer.
Sometimes in the dime store
or the library I'd lift my arm
to my nose, breathe in horse/
leather/orchard/self/other—
Steve McQueen or Charles Bronson,
some man I imagined was only
a breath a movie a century away.

Binary

Once my neck bubbled
from poison ivy.

The doctor had never seen
such a fine reaction—

so responsive, he said,
in a voice that excited me,

though I was only sixteen.
He gave my mother—who,

yes, was listening—a solution
to apply every night.

Scrub it with a popsicle
stick, he said, and she did.

I am still trying to untangle
that pleasure and pain.

Counterpoint

I started with a pretty little .22
at the shooting range next to the orchard.
My father stood behind me, coaching
Breathe, Aim, Sight, Squeeze.

I understood the order, but couldn't
concentrate on the near simultaneity
of action. *Breathe*, I thought, then
realized I was breathing but not

aiming. I needed to feather these steps
like the oars of a boat, but I had trouble
with oars, too. It was a kind
of coordination I had not developed.

I didn't slip them in right. I startled
the water. Disturbed the morning.
Breathe, Aim, Sight, Squeeze.
Row, Row, Row Your Boat.

This was *Zen*, but what did I know
of Zen except for those afternoons
I polished the spokes of my orange
ten-speed Schwinn while the Stenger

boys watched from their bedroom
window, two heads poking above the sill
like targets in a shooting gallery
at the county fair. Guns, oars, Zen,

bicycles, boys—this was my father's
concern at the range: distraction.
When anybody else showed up,
we packed our guns, buckled

the cases, left the sand pit, the pitted
target, the false dune behind the target,
and got in the truck, tuned, always,
to WKAR—Bach on the radio.

Bach with all of his counterpoint.
I was sure Bach would have handled
a gun well, would have had no problem
with *Breathe, Aim, Sight, Row.*

Bach's logic pleased my father.
What pleased my father pleased me.
The trick was how to plait
devotion & difference.

Requiem for Typewriter and a Boy from Ohio

The needle on the turntable
skips and every time I push
the return carriage a new song

starts, plays until I take the paper
out and turn it over,
and then it's Pink Floyd

did they get you to trade
your heroes for ghosts,
so I remove the paper again,

slide in a clean sheet—
twenty-five percent cotton,
static and fuzz until I start

typing, then Bruce Springsteen
and "Mary Queen of Arkansas"
and now the telephone is ringing—

it's not right to say boyfriend—
his voice whole even after 200 miles,
all the way from Cleveland

and through the gauntlet
of the phone cord, looped
like a roller coaster,

and it should be great, it should be
perfect, his voice traveling that far,
whispering in my ear, but it's not,

there is a state line between us
and a half-typed letter clamped
behind the roller, Springsteen

singing *It's not your lungs this time,*
it's your heart that holds your fate,
and the rest of the paper

above the roller sticking out
in the breeze of an open
window, ruffling.

II

The Speed of Light

After W. S. Merwin

So gradual in those summers was the going
it seemed the apples would always be
almost ripening, the pasture always
thick with clover. Days were green
with snap peas and wild tendrils.
Clematis curled through its trellis,
snapdragons bulged like the throats of frogs
until every blossom sang. I assumed
the breezy song of the veery would spiral
through every afternoon, would loop round
the orchard forever and float through
all of our days. My grandmother baked cookies,
lining the blue counter with round suns
we ate without counting. I thought
she would always only need a twenty-
minute nap, would always move like a bee
from room to room. I did not hear the soil
growing quiet. It was only at night before
sleep when I listened to my grandparents
listening to the weather radio
that I began to hear something increasing
like the height of waves, the chance of frost.

Knotweed

This morning the horses were cross
when I showed up to feed them.
They blocked the ladder to the hay mow,
would not meet my gaze.
You old stick in the mud, I said,
just like my grandfather, but they did not budge.
Still, I got their hay and fluffed the flakes
like Easter basket grass.
The horses bowed their heads, licking
their grain bins and flicking their tails.
I patted their rumps and left.

In the hospital, I saw my grandfather's legs
for the first time: purple veins hardened
like the stems of Japanese knotweed, knees
swollen like nodes on the stem.
He told me of hallucinations, how
in the fog of delirium the geometry
of this world kept bleeding angles
when he tried to define the slope of the barn.
He asked about the horses, but said only
the names of the dead ones.

Now in the amber afternoon,
they stretch their heads over the rail
and nicker. I slip under the fence
beside their skinny legs, ropy
as blue beech. I could be among trees.
How mutable, the stuff of this world.
I feed them apples, one each,
and brush them until they shine,
their lost hair blowing away,
then settling like tufts of wintered grass.

Still Life on a Train to Kalamata

He says he's from Poland,
touches my necklace, tells me
he has an apartment in Athens,
wonders if I am American.
I trace my fingers on the corner
of the passport inside my nylon pouch,
watch him stare at my neck, tell him
I am meeting a friend. I switch seats,
buy a kabob from a man waving skewers
like tiny masts of lost flags.
The meat is fused to the stick
as though to bone, but the stick
is not sharp enough to kill a goat,
not sharp enough to harm
the Polish man, who has also switched
seats, is sitting ahead of me. He asks
about my watch, my travel plans.
He wants to see my passport,
my credit card. The train is moving faster,
the man selling kabobs is swaying in the aisle,
the Polish man's questions are flying
out his window, blowing back in my window.
His voice, when it reenters, is coated with dust
and something red, maybe poppies
from the field outside, maybe blood
from a skewered goat, maybe the silk stripe
of a flag that does not wave to him.
It is a color that ought to be painted
with a fat ox-hair brush
because we are moving fast,
the Polish man is sweating, the kabob man
is sweating, I am sweating.
Everything is blurry,
smeared into one crimson, impressionistic
smudge until the only firm, fixed
thing in the scene is the stag-handled knife
in my pocket, the single blade
folded inside like a secret.

Chisel & Wave

I used to crack rocks open with a cold chisel
to find what hid inside. Even now, I keep

a split geode on the mantle. When I hold it
to my ear, I hear a boy in college confiding

he'd called my name in his sleep, camping:
my name on his lips, my name floating

in the Beartooth Mountains above
alpine buttercups and saxifrage.

For years, I imagined secrets were shared
by pressing two ears together, sealing them

so news traveled out of one into another,
a secure transaction. I was almost right—

close to understanding the waves that pass
between flesh and flesh.

Strike

My nephew flies a drone
over my grandparents' empty house,
over the orchard and empty barn,
and past glazed windows—sun igniting
the stained wallpaper of empty rooms.
Every day the temperature slips—
minus five, minus ten, and still
the fire department plots to burn the house.
We wait for the match to strike—
a flame as slender as a finger.
They'll bring in hay bales and wood
pallets to kindle what is empty.
It hardly makes sense, the scale
of what will come. My grandpa
lit one match each autumn, put a log
on the fire every night before bed,
stoked the fire every morning
with apple wood until apple trees
blossomed in May. He kept his fires
small, cleaned his chimney.
My nephew flies the drone
with insect certainty—sends it
through the breezeway and over
flagstone steps, and for a moment
it's my grandma—alive, running—
her boots, unbuckled,
flapping past the picket fence.
Then her arms are wings again,
she's 400 feet above the back door,
and I stand in snow and ice, knowing
how heat will rise, that hawks
will glide on thermals.

Fire Department Exercise

Up in the rafters,
a panicked raccoon freezes
on a crossbeam.

It has pilfered
baling twine, latch to
the grain bin, buckle

from a pony's harness,
owl egg from a nest
in the eaves. Even its

scat—clumps hardened
on empty pallets, caked
on a windowsill—steals

the scent of hay.
It won't make it out, but look
at what escapes:

swallows sweeping across
a slate sky, their felted
wings wiping out gnats,

pollen, words that still
linger—*goodnight old girls,
stay warm*. Almost

a movie scene, this barn
burning, but it's only a fire
department exercise.

No one will run out
in long johns to save any
animals. There aren't

any actors—grandfather
calling *Ruthie, Dolly*, grandmother
pressing two sugar cubes

into the palm of my hand.
The horses are dead,
buried in mounds beside

the barn, eye sockets stuffed
with dirt, bones sunk too deep
for coyotes to pick.

Later, for hours, plumes
of smoke will swirl
like chalk dust,

raccoons will raise
tiny, leather hands
and wave goodbye.

The Eternal Return

After W. S. Merwin

Because it is not here it is eternal
how else to explain the absence
of the moon in the afternoon
the disappearance of loons
in September the silence
when I wake at night that time
between the last sound
of the last frog and the first
sound of the first ice
where does anything go except
into forever my grandmother
comes to me at night is always
waiting at the end of the hallway
in a house that is not there
by the heavy black-corded telephone
in the nook by the closet
where her jacket still hangs

Prelude to an Elegy, 18,000 Feet

The No Smoking sign glows like a little flame,
flickers when the plane drops. I'm nowhere
above somewhere, rows of seat backs

like tombstones, waiting for a wing to rip,
waiting to fall cockeyed through a cloud—
trail of ash, evidence rinsed by rain.

A girl next to me, maybe twenty, clings
to the knee of a girl next to her—
a terrifying age to die. Only a few

minutes ago they were flipping
through catalogs, pointing at blouses.
Now I imagine they imagine clothes

spilling from suitcases, a dress
that might catch in a tree, billow like a girl
dancing alone until even the wind dies.

Cosmic Memory I

Sometimes I see my grandmother
two streets away from my house,
in a house where she lived in college.
I found the address in her book—

Flowers East of the Rockies—the street
printed in blurry ink. I like to walk
at night and look for her in the amber
square of an unshuttered window.

One night, I watched her comb
her hair. My own scalp prickled,
tingled more when she turned
and we stared at each other,

my breath rising, evaporating
in the orange halo of a streetlight.
I walked home, stood in front
of my bedroom mirror and waited

to see her. Later, sewing a button
on a wool coat, I found a drop
of dried blood just before I pricked
myself with the needle. I licked

my finger and it tasted exactly as it did
eighty-seven years before when she,
trying to buckle a mare's bridle,
cut her thumb on the throatlatch.

After Two Weeks Alone, I Visit the Harvard Museum of Natural History

Here beetles are arranged like a color wheel,
hung like a dartboard, like
pin the tail on the donkey,
except the beetles are already pinned
and there is glass between us,
glass in front of the Bengal tiger,
glass in front of the hunk of goethite
from Negaunee, Michigan.
I wander from Asia to Africa
to Thoreau's Maine woods,
between continents separated
not by water, not by mountains.
Later, outside, I roam neighborhoods,
every block an exhibit.
At a playground on Oxford Street,
girls dangle upside down, their hair spreading
like roots from the hart's-tongue fern,
glass flower behind a case.
Across the street, a café
where I see my reflection—
my orange shorts, my two legs—
fixed in the window. I stop.
The tread of my sandal leaves no footprint,
yet here is my likeness, shell of myself.
I look at the girls blooming
on the trellis of the playground.
Tonight I do not know
which side of the glass I am on.
Mothers are plucking daughters
from latticed monkey bars.
The barista locks the door of the café.
I walk to my rented room,
open every window, watch a cat
slink down the street. When I crawl in bed,
the slim beam of a streetlight
pins me to my sheets.

Ember

"I move so easily into a sermon." —John Cage

Afternoons my grandfather hitched
the mare to the cutter—bridle and bit,
breast collar, breeches, traces, crupper—
the horse stomping as my grandfather bent
to cinch the girth, adjust a trace, climb
into the seat, untwist the reins—lurch
of the cutter when he flicked them.
Then the mare kicking snow, the world
quiet except for the slip of runners, squeak
of leather rubbing on a shaft, the breath
of a horse in winter, an orchard gone
silent—anechoic chamber.
I could hear my own blood.

In another winter, I am the horse
that pulls my son in a sled between
scrub oaks. My son, swaddled
in a quilt, draws silence into the hold
of himself—his head so full of quiet
it floats, untethered, even as the rope
around my waist tightens and I lean
into the wind, push harder through knee-
deep silence, through white paintings—
snow so light it can't make it to earth,
keeps swirling like ash stirred
from a fire long cold.

Pictograph

Trans-Canada Highway, Lake Superior Provincial Park, Ontario

By August, the bears have learned again
the use of roads, how they lead
to campgrounds, campgrounds to food.

One is ambling north along the shoulder,
plump and careless. I am on the other shoulder,
between a guardrail and a Chevy Blazer,

then between guardrail and bear,
between guardrail and semitrailer,
eighteen wheels kicking stones

into my spokes, my fingers squeezed
around handlebars. This road
is no place for a bicycle, but I pedal

and estimate how far I'd plummet
before hitting a granite boulder,
how the bloody imprint of my body

on gray rock might be washed by rain,
licked by bears, my carcass ravaged
by buzzards. I have come

from the pictographs near the mouth
of the Agawa River, have seen
Mishipeshu, the Great Lynx,

keeper of Lake Superior. *Scaled tail,*
reptile in the shape of a cat, tobacco
and sweetgrass. I know there is more

to lasting art than the shape of a body
or red ochre mixed with bear
grease and the varnish of what leaches

from rock. I can't render
transcendence—am not made
of anything that will survive.

Die-Cast

Highway 1, Marin County

The blue rug was water.
I propped a yardstick over it—
one end of the stick on the raised hearth,
one end on the wood floor, the rug
in between. I pushed matchbox cars
down—witnessed them slide off,
plummet upside down, windshields
skidding like hockey pucks—
recorded how far they made it,
which side of the stick each car slid off,
when a car flipped and landed right-side up,
stunt-like—James Bond nailing
the Astro Spiral Jump. Physics,
statistics, tricks. Nothing of flesh
or sorrow. I scooped those cars up,
blessed them.

Now I'm in a rental car, a Dodge Caliber
with bad brakes, not enough land
to fit a guardrail—just the road
and not the road, then the ocean
a few hundred feet below, rolling
like an oil slick. I'm driving toward
an unlabeled future, passing other cars
with drivers headed toward other futures
and, no, this is not like a story problem.
There is no *A* or *B*, no train, no fixed
speed, but maybe, yes, an *x* axis, a *y* axis,
metaphysics, fortunes, past actions.
The narrow road, bad tires, sloppy
steering. I imagine faceless drivers
who abused this car, what might be
loose or broken—joints, tie-rod, gears.
I count miles, look for skid marks, wait
for that place I'll veer off—my body spinning

in the body of a spinning black Caliber,
a child standing in the sand, penciling
numbers on a yellow notepad, a little god
in Toughskins and a Faygo T-shirt
squinting into the sun, wondering
how to measure the accident.

Lake Shore in Half Light

After W. S. Merwin

There is a question I want to ask,
and I don't trust a Ouija board
to even ask what it is, and God,
I think, already knows but is waiting
for me to better form it on my own.
Rilke urged his young correspondent
to live the questions and, by living them,
live into the answers, and so
I worry if I can't form the question
I might not even be living. I have spent
long evenings soaking in the bathtub,
trying to soften the question,
coax it out like a splinter.
I've come to suspect the question
is somewhere outside of myself.
Here on the lake shore in half light
I am waiting for it to float to me
like an old log washed ashore.
I will scoop it up and bring it,
dripping, back to my towel. I will
swaddle it like a cold child and
carry it wherever it needs to go.

Far Company

After W. S. Merwin

At times now from some margin of the day
I can smell apples cooking in a pan,
for a moment cinnamon or maybe only
the memory of cinnamon until all of it
blows away and I am left remembering
not apples but what apples help me
remember—my grandmother at the stove,
her apron tied behind her into a bow,
the bow like a swallowtail, and I'm afraid
if I move I'll spook the butterfly,
but I move anyway—there is no way to make
anything last—and then I'm outside
another house with another open window
where the scent of apples has floated
and settled in a pot of bubbling oatmeal,
and my mind, which like a child
had stayed behind to remember
the calico print of the cotton apron,
clambers up behind me, tugs
my jacket sleeve, and wonders if
we should walk home to the garden
and wait by the zinnias.

There Was a Child Went Forth

This morning the president speaks to me
through a wood-cased radio in Michigan.
Orange peels cook in a tin can on the stove.

I lace my boots, hang my skates around
my neck. Somewhere on a range not far,
the National Guard drops bombs

into a sand pit. But it's eleven degrees
and sunny. It's the day after Christmas.
I'm halfway to the rink at the end of the lake,

my blades polished by a boy at the hardware
store too young to serve but old enough
to hone a metal edge knife-sharp,

when an F-16 cuts into my silence, flies
over, circles back. Two hundred thousand
acres of military land, and I am a flash & speck

of myself. I think of a deer a few yards
from my rink—run down, circled.
Rack of bones and blood-soaked snow.

Coyote tracks. But I'm more than a doe.
I'm Whitman's child—radio and orange rind,
a child gone forth. And I'm skating faster now,

carving glass etchings, hieroglyphics,
arabesques, waving to my pilot,
who does what his radio commands.

Untouched

After W. S. Merwin

Even in dreams if I am there I keep trying
    to walk the streets of an old neighborhood,
keep listening for a cello recital I left after intermission.
    One snowy night a bartender gave me
a bowl of warm bread pudding. *On me,*
    he said after I praised the Bolognese,
and I am still sorry I pushed the dollop
    of ice cream aside. The last time I had
coffee at the corner café I left a waxed print of my parted
    lips on a blue mug, like a cloud.
When I closed the door on a dormered room
    above the city I left the shower dripping,
every *plink* the measure of a second, gone.
    I left chimney swifts twittering in the eaves,
petals of dandelions opening to a new day.
    I left the dew on the bracken ferns
in Mount Auburn Cemetery and left
    moss growing over the gravestone
of a drummer boy, rhizoids creeping
    into the etched grooves of his name.

Vanitas

A cobweb blows in a wind
I can't feel. When I reach
to still it, my finger catches

in a gap, silk circle that looks
like a phone dial. I call
my mother. No answer.

I call my sister—breath
whistling in an acorn cap.
I'm standing in the rain

near the end of a hike, one leg
stretched on a boulder, the other
arrow-straight, fixed

between dirt and noon sun.
I look like a clock, but I can't
gauge anything—the head

of a queen I cannot name
carved in the burl of an oak,
my grandmother's knuckle

swollen into a gall. A half a mile
later I find the skull of a fox
skewered on a fence post, water

dripping through eye sockets.
All of that silence inside.
I run my finger over teeth,

wiggle a molar and—trick
of memory—I am eight, standing
in front of a cracked mirror trying

to see what my tongue already
knows. I rub the mandible,
flinch from my own cold fingers.

Trying to Pray

After James Wright

This time, I have left my body behind me
and stepped out of it as though slipping
out of a pair of hip waders, noting the miracle
of my dry feet and the shape of something
I once inhabited collapsing. In my sorrow
I am as pale and soft-bodied as an insect
after loosening itself from itself.
Isn't this how they do it, the mantises?

My Hand

After W. S. Merwin

See how the past is not finished—
my son, home for a visit, talking
as he leashes his dog, and it is
the voice of my grandfather
coaxing his mare into a halter
and then I'm waving goodbye to him
just as my grandparents waved, as
my parents waved, and back
in the house there is the saddle
that came with my dad's first
horse, Smokey, and now
the saddle is on a walnut stand
in my living room, horseless,
riderless, though the leather still
creaks near the quarter strap ring
as though feet are still in the stirrups.
When I move my hand to quiet the squeak
my fingers brush a warm flank,
but when I reach again to pat
the flank there's only air and my hand
is only a gesture in the air, low, the way
one adjusts the arm to wave
goodbye to a child.

Digital

Rothko's Harvard Murals faded while on display in the 1960s and 1970s. They were removed in 1979 and stored for decades. In 2014, an exhibition at the Fogg Museum returned them to a public space. The exhibit used digital projection to restore the appearance of the original colors.

Somewhere, a curator sits in a booth
cranking a dial until Rothko's murals drip.

I almost believe it—this science
of calculated healing or calibrated

bleeding, this world as hologram,
my own body as pixels and light,

modulated ecstasy. Still, I spin
my own dial. I am my own

curator. Rothko mixed his own
pigments, watched Lithol red

stain his fingers. And when I touch
the sleeve of a friend, it's flannel

I think I feel, not an idea of flannel.
Touch me. Tell me this world

is more than what we fix,
prove that your flesh is real.

Nocturne

After W. S. Merwin

August arrives in the dark,
carried on the wings of insects.
I am halfway up the stairs to bed
when I hear them—a chorus as sudden
as mushrooms after rain. Every summer
I wonder how I never notice
what has been coming until a night
when I climb the stairs to an opened window
or leave a friend's after a late dinner
and step outside to a world tipped
toward autumn and walk home wistful
for June nights when summer was still
a little green ball on an unstaked plant
waiting to ripen.

Willow City Loop, Texas

The armadillos on the side of the road
wear leather and chain mail.

Some of them are infected
with leprosy. Pastures are full

of fire ants and rattlesnakes,
the land sewn with barbed wire.

I've heard ranchers will shoot
if you trespass. Still, I like it here,

driving with the windows down
in April, bluebonnets and Texas

mountain laurel blooming
like pieces of the sky. Inside

the general store, men gather
at a table next to candy and fly swatters.

Their faces lift like the heads
of spooked cattle. We nod.

One resumes eating a sandwich,
another shuffles a deck of cards.

The beer cooler hums,
and even the flies are still again

in the dust of windows. I've come
for one beer, but I buy a six-pack,

pull five bottles of Shiner Bock—
gold labels glossed with dew—

set them in the middle of the table
like a bouquet of wildflowers.

Kettle

Yesterday I heard the kettle's shrill
whistle calling the rabbits home
for tea. I turned the burner off, but
it kept calling, and it sounded just like
the water in my grandma's kettle
when it was time to feed the birds.
There is something about my ear
that is always tuned to the past.
Here's a story I don't remember
anymore: when I was little
I used to drink out of puddles,
my tongue a rainbow
of rainwater and gasoline.
If you looked at the country inside me,
you would see whole pastures
overgrown with box elder and grapevines.
I've written you twenty-five songs.
Can you hear me singing?

These Are the Nights That Beetles Love

It is true these are the nights
that beetles love. And these days,
and mornings, too. August
is their favorite month.
They have tracked the moon's
orbit, checked the temperature
of sand and gravel, measured
the angle of the sun on the ferns
and noted how it looks,
this evening, like a picture of sun
on ferns. They know nobody
you love is in the hospital.
They know your parents
are still alive. When you sit down
with a bowl of orange sherbet
and pause to consider the shape
of sunshine on the porch floor,
some general in their army
of beetles—Japanese, June,
cucumber, carpet, carrion,
dung, blister, powderpost—
orders one armored creature,
little tank, to rumble across
the floor in front of you, right
into the trapezoid of sunshine
you have waited all summer
to feel on your feet in this moment
after dinner when you thought
the world was perfect.

Forgotten Streams

After W. S. Merwin

The names of unimportant streams have fallen
off like shelves of ice into stronger currents.
For a while a few curled around the leaves
of eelgrass, hid in silt, clung to moss
on slippery boulders. Then they were
vowelless, scoured, dissolved.
We can't even pan for them anymore.
When I open my mouth to name a few
it's just air rushing out of a dry canyon.
What was the creek where my father
floated on lost summer days—
a swimming hole under a canopy of maples,
gone now along with the name, but which
went first, name or hole, and what
was the name of the stream his grandfather
fished and will I be the last person in the world
to say the name of my grandmother's brother,
dead at thirteen from pneumonia, gone more
than a century, *Theron*. There, I've said it.
Take the name with you. Carry it like a seed.

Some Nights

Some nights the coyotes sing for hours,
their chorus a twist of feral monks
and Warren Zevon howling
in a grove of jack pines. Sometimes
I think what I hear is my own breath
coming back to me, recycled, upcycled,
mixed with dry needles, dust,
oil from an eagle's tail feather. Still,
the breath is mine—it holds the shape
of my lungs, and from it I gather verbs
I gave up months ago: *listen*
carve, float. Imagine—a song, a knife,
a river coming back. Once, I woke up
holding a harmonica in my hand,
wondering if I cooked that music myself.

Replica in Helium & Ether

Late September in a fire tower above
bugling elk, and I'm drinking tea
with my father—steam rising

from the cup as though I've brought
my own smoke for the red-tipped
maples, my own liquid for the river.

Some days my body floats free
of itself. It's not just the soul, but
all of myself detached from itself—

one self hovering like a balloon,
and one reckoning the angle
of the sun. Here above autumn,

the trick is not how to keep
one aloft, but how to coax
a shadow back into the body.

Antique Sound

After W. S. Merwin

There was an age when you played records
made from shellac, and later there was another
of vinyl, but these days I play topo maps
cut into twelve-inch discs, glued together
to form two sides. I've been playing
one map of an old orchard over and over,
listening to the music of blossoms
and the sound of the eastern ridge
where the orchard ended. When I flip
the map I can hear the crinkle of frost
crystallizing below that ridge, the sound
of the river beyond the orchard.
On the steep slope above the river
is a thicket of grapevines,
and when the map spins fast enough
I can hear the tags on the collar of a beagle
jingle. She's flushed a rabbit and soon
she'll appear, her ears bleeding from briars.
I am close to being there. I am stretched
out on the floor with my eyes closed
just like a teenager, but the album ends
too soon, as the best records do.
When this one wears out, as it will,
I'll cut a thin cross section from the stump
of an old apple tree, and I will play the rings
through cambium, sapwood, and heartwood
until the needle finds the pith.

NOTES

My grandparents' farm, mentioned in many poems in this book, was east of Grand Ledge, Michigan, along and above the Grand River. Some of that land is now Hunter's Orchard Park.

When a poem in this book includes an epigraph acknowledging W. S. Merwin, the poem uses the title and first line of Merwin's poem.

"There Was a Child Went Forth" borrows its title from Walt Whitman.

"Trying to Pray" borrows its title from James Wright's poem and uses most of Wright's first line.

"These Are the Nights That Beetles Love" borrows its title from a poem by Emily Dickinson.

ACKNOWLEDGMENTS

Thanks are due to the editors of the following publications, in which some of the poems first appeared:

32 Poems
"Antique Sound"

The American Journal of Poetry
"Ember"

Chautauqua
"Rain Light"

Diode
"These Are the Nights That Beetles Love"

The Harlequin
"Fire Department Exercise"
"Willow City Loop, Texas"
"Knotweed"

Juked
"Still Life on a Train to Kalamata"

Lily Poetry Review
"Kettle"
"Replica in Helium & Ether"

North Dakota Quarterly
"Digital"

The Pinch
"Cosmic Memory I"
"Centaur"

Salt Hill
"Nocturne"

Stirring
"Requiem for Typewriter and a Boy from Ohio"

Tinderbox Poetry Journal
"1978" (previously titled "Feral")
"Prelude to an Elegy, 18,000 Feet"

♦ ♦ ♦

Filmmaker Peter Johnston adapted "Cosmic Memory I" for a short film that premiered at the MSU Filmetry Festival at Michigan State University in January 2019.

♦ ♦ ♦

As ever, I share thanks with my parents, Tom and Nancy Hunter, and my son, Tommy Morgan. They've made their own art in their own ways and encouraged me as I've made mine. Thanks also to my larger family for all the days we shared in the orchard and for the times we've spent walking, wandering, and camping in Michigan. Many of these poems grew from those times and those places.

Thanks to friends from Lesley University's MFA program, particularly Steven Cramer, Kevin Prufer, Cate Marvin, Eileen Cleary, Robbie Gamble, Jon D. Lee, Mani Iyer, Michael Mercurio, Andrea Read, Christine Jones, and Suzanne Edison.

◆　◆　◆

Special thanks to Terri Miller, who believes in books and libraries and has supported me again and again, and thanks to all my colleagues at MSU Libraries who help collect and share books. Gracious appreciation for friends who share various and important parts of their lives in various and important ways: Maureen Abood, Eric Alstrom, Jenn Arbogast, Ken Bigger, Renae Bradley, Janine Certo, Larry Cosentino, Stacy Dickert-Conlin, Shanna Draheim, Jodi Eppinga, Marcus Fields, Julie Marshall Garcia, Karin Gottshall, Katy Hennessy, Karen Henry, Dennis Hinrichsen, Peter Johnston, Joan Jolly, Arie Koelewyn, Annette Kopachik, Geralyn Lasher, Julie Laxton, Thomas Lynch, Jen Novello, Tessa Paneth-Pollak, Carol Pratt, Sarah Preisser, Steve Rachman, Philip Rice, Meg Ropp, Jennifer Rosa, Dave Sheridan, Anita Skeen, John Smolens, Julie Stivers, Karen Marshall Wischmeyer, and Chris Worland. Finally, many thanks to Annie Martin at Wayne State University Press for believing in my work, and thanks to all at Wayne State University Press who help to bring books into the world.

ABOUT THE AUTHOR

CINDY HUNTER MORGAN is the author of *Harbor-less* (Wayne State University Press), which was a 2018 Michigan Notable Book and the winner of the 2017 Moveen Prize in Poetry. She also is the author of two chapbooks, *Apple Season* (Midwest Writing Center Chapbook Award, 2012) and *The Sultan, The Skater, The Bicycle Maker* (Ledge Press Chapbook Award, 2011). She taught poetry, creative writing, and book arts at Michigan State University for several years and now heads up communications for Michigan State University Libraries. She is a co-founder of the MSU Filmetry Festival, an annual event showcasing short films adapted from poems, and she leads various poetry workshops and book arts workshops.